Simple Solutions™
Obedience

By Kim Campbell Thornton
Illustrations by Buck Jones

Plus Training Tips

BOWTIE PRESS®

IRVINE, CALIFORNIA

Nick Clemente, Special Consultant
Karla Austin, Business Operations Manager
Ruth Strother, Editor-at-Large
Michelle Martinez, Editor
Michael Vincent Capozzi, Designer

The dogs in this book are referred to as *he* and *she* in alternating chapters.

Library of Congress Cataloging-in-Publication Data

Thornton, Kim Campbell.
  Simple solutions : obedience / by Kim Campbell Thornton ;
illustrations by Buck Jones.
     p. cm.
  ISBN 1-931993-09-2 (pbk. : alk. paper)
  1. Dogs--Training. 2. Dogs--Behavior. I. Title.

  SF431.T534 2003
  636.7'0887--dc21

                              2003004492

BowTie Press®
A Division of BowTie, Inc.
3 Burroughs
Irvine, California 92618
949-855-8822

Printed and Bound in Singapore
10 9 8 7 6 5 4 3 2

Contents

Petiquette for Pooches

Some dogs wouldn't dream of challenging their people, while others are gunning for the top spot from the first day they walk into the house. It's important to know your dog and to establish yourself as her leader early on in the relationship. Not by being mean or bossy to the dog, but by being consistent in all your actions so she learns to work with and respect you.

The formal training of puppy kindergarten and obedience school are only one step toward teaching your dog to become a civilized member of the family. Classroom

training is important, but it isn't enough to ensure that your dog becomes a successful member of human society.

In addition to classroom training, dogs need plenty of interaction with the world around them, a process known as socialization. Rewards, such as praise and treats, when they do the right thing (so they know to repeat those desirable behaviors); an understanding of their place in the family pack; and—as with all lessons throughout life—practice, practice, practice are key in socializing your dog.

Because every human family is different, we all have different behaviors we want to teach our dogs. Nonetheless, the obedience lessons covered here will help your dog to be welcome both in your home and in public places.

Who's the Boss?

Teaching manners is important not only for harmonious living, but also to establish yourself as your dog's leader. When dogs live together they have a pack leader who decides when everyone eats and how much they get; where everyone sleeps; when playtime begins and ends; what kind of play will take place; what to investigate on the trail; and so on. Now that your dog lives with you, he needs you to be the pack leader and make those kinds of decisions for him. If you don't, he'll try to take over the role himself, and that's not good.

Part of establishing leadership is teaching your dog to obey commands and how to behave in the house and around people. Be firm but not harsh. Avoid using discredited techniques such as alpha rolls—forcing the dog onto his back and staring at him—which are dangerous and ineffective. Instead, be consistent with what you ask of your dog and insist that he comply—as long as you're sure he understands what you want.

The Social Graces of the Urbane Dog

A happy, confident dog loves meeting people, plays well with other dogs, acts politely toward cats, and shows curiosity rather than fearfulness when encountering unfamiliar objects. When a dog has these attributes, she's said to be well socialized. A well-socialized dog isn't born, though; she's made. There's no doubt that a dog's personality is important, but unless you make the effort to introduce Duchess to all kinds of people, places, and

things at an early age, she will never reach her full social potential, and that would be a shame.

The critical period in a young pup's life is from three to fourteen weeks of age. That's when her brain is most open to new experiences. Older dogs benefit from socialization as well. It may take them a little longer to become accustomed to new things, but they can learn. Socialize them the same way you would a puppy. Remember, the most important factors that contribute to the making of a happy, confident dog are socialization and an understanding of her place within her human family.

For a well-adjusted dog, expose your pup in a positive way to people of all ages and appearances: people wearing hats or glasses; people on skateboards and bicycles; and people using wheelchairs or walkers. Introduce her to the sounds of vacuum cleaners, lawn mowers, electronic toys, and any other noises she may commonly encounter.

Take Duchess to public places where dogs are welcome such as parks, pet supply stores, and—of course—the veterinary clinic and grooming shop. A lot of places permit well-behaved dogs, so keep it that way by taking your dog on leash and controlling her behavior in public.

Your attitude is the key to a confident dog. If Duchess sees that you're relaxed about a person's approach or a noise that's being made, she will follow your lead. Conversely, if she senses that you're anxious, she'll become anxious herself.

The veterinary clinic is a great place to start socializing your dog. Schedule an appointment for an exam or weight check only—no painful needles, please! Walk your dog into the clinic with a smile on your face, and let the staff greet her with pats and treats. If she seems fearful, don't try to soothe her by crooning that it's okay. That simply confirms her belief that something awful awaits her. Just ignore her. Let her explore at her own pace; don't pick her up or force her toward staff members. Praise her when she investigates on her own, and ignore her if she's cowering under a chair. When Duchess is being brave or at least calm, praise her and give a treat. Repeat these just-for-fun vet visits as often as possible; there's no charge for bringing your dog to the clinic to be weighed and then giving her a treat.

Use this same technique anytime you take Duchess someplace new or introduce her to someone. Keep treats

on hand so strangers can give one to Duchess when they meet. If your dog is reluctant to approach a new person, lay a trail of treats to him or her so Duchess can move toward the new person gradually—not to mention happily.

And remember—never force your dog to go toward someone: Fearful dogs bite! This advice applies to both large and small dogs. In fact, it's even more important for small dogs, because our first instinct is to pick them up and cuddle them. Don't do it. Small dogs need to develop confidence just as much as large ones do—maybe even more so.

It's just as important for you to socialize Duchess with other dogs as it is for you to socialize her with other people. Training class is a great place for Duchess to meet other dogs. Some classes divide pups into groups of large and small dogs, but make sure your dog gets a chance to mix with dogs of all sizes and breeds. If she's big, she needs to learn to step carefully around small dogs, and if she's small she needs to learn to have confidence around her larger brethren.

Other good places to meet dogs are at parks. Plan a play date with friends and their dogs. Because parks are neutral terrain—they don't "belong" to any one dog—territorial disagreements are less likely to break out. Supervise the interactions until you're sure the dogs are getting along.

Beauty Is As Beauty Does

One of the signs of a nice dog is that he's willing to be petted or handled by many different people. This is important because it makes grooming, veterinary care, and participation in dog sports much easier. Willingness to be handled is a by-product of socialization. The dog who meets a lot of people learns to expect petting in a variety of situations. He learns that touch is pleasant, not frightening.

Start accustoming Duke to being handled for grooming and veterinary care when he's a puppy. Take him in your lap and gently brush him. Speak softly to him, saying things

such as "That feels good, doesn't it, Duke?" Lift up his ears

and look inside them. Run your fingers around the inside

of his lips. Stroke his paws and then pick them up and hold them. Although most dogs hate having their feet handled, they can learn to tolerate it if you start early enough and are persistent. A good time for these handling sessions is while you're watching TV.

At first, handle Duke for only a minute or two at a time, then gradually extend the length of time you spend grooming him. When he's used to having your fingers in his mouth, introduce him to a soft dog toothbrush. You'll be thankful for all of your prep work when his coat grows out and needs frequent combing or when he needs a bath.

Sitting Pretty

The *sit* command is one of the easiest to teach and one of the most useful. Pups can learn it at an early age, so it's a great way to accustom them to the training process. Requiring your dog to sit is also a great way to reinforce your status as the leader.

The first thing Duchess should learn is that she gets attention when she sits. Not when she jumps up. Not when she runs away. When she sits. Because *sit* is often the first command dogs learn, it seems to stick more firmly in their brain, and they often respond to it more readily

than to any other command. That's why it has so many great uses.

To teach the *sit* command, start by getting Duchess's attention. Show her a treat and slowly move it upward so she has to raise her head to see it. Most dogs naturally move into a sitting position when they do this. If Duchess isn't quite there, gently push down on her rump while moving your hand back over her head to give her the idea. When she's in position tell her to sit and give her the treat. Practice for only a couple of minutes (puppies have a short attention span) and repeat several times throughout the day. Soon Duchess will recognize that your uplifted hand signals the *sit* command even if you're not holding a treat.

Practice using the *sit* command in different situations once Duchess associates it with the action of sitting. Teach her to sit and wait before you pet her, before you feed her, and before you put her leash on. If you're out in the yard and she wanders away from you tell her to sit so she learns to respond even when you're at a distance. This won't be helpful if she's at risk of being hit by a car, but it can be useful in a more controlled situation when you simply want her to wait for you. (A leash, of course, is the

best way to keep a dog under control and should always be used in unfamiliar or unfenced areas.)

To teach the *wait* or *stay* command, place your dog in a sit. Hold up your hand, with the flat of your palm toward the dog's face, and tell her to wait or stay (whichever you prefer); then back up a few steps. If your dog remains where she is, praise her. Gradually increase the amount of time she must wait before receiving praise or a reward. If she moves out of place, don't punish her, simply put her back in position and start over.

Jumping Up

Jumping is one of the most common complaints people have about their dogs. It may be cute when a puppy does it, but a couple of months later, when his size has doubled, it can become a problem. You don't want Duke knocking down Aunt Mary or Baby Sue with his exuberant greeting. Replace jumping behavior as soon as possible with the *sit* command.

Teaching a dog not to jump up doesn't require any harsh tactics. Ignore anyone who tells you to knee the dog in the chest or push him away. Instead, simply pivot

so he misses you. Then give the *sit* command. When Duke

complies, give him a lot of praise or a treat. Repeat this

every time he tries to jump up and insist that other people do so as well.

Often, especially with toy breeds, people say that they don't mind, and refuse to participate in the training process. If you have a large dog, that's not really an option because you don't want to run the risk of someone being injured, even inadvertently. It's not so bad with a toy breed, but remember that even small dogs can snag your stockings or scratch your legs when they jump up. It's better if you teach them the same good manners you would teach a larger dog.

On or Off the Furniture?

Lying on furniture or sleeping in bed is practically a given for the modern dog, but it should be a privilege rather than a right. Decide before you get a dog whether you want to allow her on the furniture at all or if you want to limit her to specific pieces of furniture or even to her own dog bed on the floor. In this matter there's no right or wrong decision, but it is one that you need to make and implement from day one so Duchess doesn't become confused.

The advantage to letting your dog on the furniture is that she's fun to snuggle with while you're reading or

watching TV. Dogs are our best friends, after all. The dis-

advantage is that dogs leave hair and skin oils behind,

which can make your furniture look shabby in no time flat. If you want to cuddle with Duchess but still keep your sofa looking nice, you can compromise by covering it with a sheet or slipcover, or by laying down a blanket in a certain area and limiting your dog to that spot. You may also teach her that she's permitted only on certain pieces of furniture. For instance, the old sofa in the den is okay, but not the brocade one in the living room.

If you don't want Duchess on the furniture at all, never let her up on it—not even once. If she tries to get on the bed or sofa with you, take her to her bed or other designated area and tell her to stay. You will have to repeat this many times, but it will eventually sink in.

What about sleeping with you? A lot of trainers and behaviorists advise against this, saying that it gives the dog an overblown opinion of herself and can lead to problems with aggression. Again, because each dog is an individual, there is no right or wrong answer here. By establishing yourself as your dog's leader early on, she will learn to work with and respect you.

Mealtime Manners

Most dogs are highly motivated by food. When they know dinner's being prepared (yours or theirs), they may dance around, jump up on you, and otherwise get underfoot. While this is cute to watch (at least the first couple of times), it's not really the best behavior to permit in the kitchen, where you run the risk of stepping on Duke or dropping a hot pan because you tripped over him. Nor do you want a dog who practically snatches the food dish out of your hand as you're setting it down. The kitchen, then, is a great place for your dog to practice the *sit* command.

If you're preparing food, put your dog in a sit stay in an out-of-the-way corner. He can still watch; he just won't be in the way. As with any command, be consistent. You can't let your dog roam the kitchen sometimes and then expect him to understand why he's all of a sudden not allowed to.

Require your dog to sit before meals as well. This keeps him from jumping up and wolfing down his food. Because canine manners wither away if they're not used, this is a good way to get in a quick practice session twice a day.

Feed your dog before the rest of the family eats. Behaviorists now say that a well-fed dog is less likely to become anxious about guarding his food. He's also less likely to beg at the table, a bad habit that should be strong- ly discouraged. While the family eats, tell your dog to go to his

place. Make sure the kids and your spouse don't slip him their veggies under the table; that only encourages begging behavior. Some dogs make a practice of lying beneath the baby's high chair, having learned that it's where manna falls from the heavens. Dogs are good vacuum cleaners, so you may not mind this if you have an especially messy baby, but be aware that it reinforces the begging habit. Decide now which is more important to you: a clean floor or a dog who doesn't beg.

Come When Called

Come is the most important command Duchess will ever learn. Use it to call her for meals, for playtime, for bedtime, and—most importantly—for taking her out of harm's way. When Duchess is about to run right in front of a speeding car and you scream at her to come and she responds instantly, you've just saved her life. If you don't teach your dog anything else, teach her to come when you call.

The *come* command is fun to teach because there's no way Duchess can mess it up. She's always going to get praise or a treat when she comes to you. Start teaching

the *come* command on the first day you bring your puppy

or dog home. Puppies instinctively follow people. Use that

instinct to your advantage. Make eye contact with your puppy and in your happiest, most excited tone of voice tell her to come. When she gets to you, make a big fuss and praise her.

Another way to get your dog excited about coming is to rattle a box of treats as you call her. Use something really good-smelling such as cat treats so she'll think it's worthwhile to head your way. Practice several times every day in different places. Anytime your dog heads toward you on her own, use it as a training opportunity. Tell her to come and praise and reward her when she gets to you.

Practice the *come* command when you're playing in the yard, holding Duchess's favorite toy. Instead of chasing

Duchess, teach her to chase you. Hold treats or a toy and run away from her. As she takes off after you, tell her to come. When she catches you, praise her. Tell Duchess to come when she follows you into the kitchen to prepare her meal. If you're a whistler, whistle a particular tune as you set down the food. If you can't whistle, try ringing a bell. Like Pavlov's dogs, Duchess will learn to come running every time she hears that melody.

Don't give the *come* command if you can't enforce it. Anytime Duchess doesn't come when you call, go and get her. Then walk her back to where you called her, telling

her to come along the way and praising her when you get back to where you started.

Another way to do this is to practice the *come* command while your dog is wearing a leash. That way, if she doesn't come when you call, you can use the leash to enforce the command.

Never act angry when you're practicing the *come* command; you want Duchess to always be happy about coming to you. Never yell at your dog after she has come to you or call her and then do something unpleasant. If you need to give her a bath or trim her nails, go and get her.

No Marking Please!

Dogs are territorial animals, staking their claim to particular areas or objects in a variety of ways. One of these ways is urine-marking—Duke lifts his leg and squirts a shot of urine on the valued area. (Female dogs may also urine-mark and some even lift a leg to do so.) Most dogs do this outside on trees or light poles where it isn't a big deal, but sometimes they bring this behavior into the home where it's not acceptable at all. Your dog needs to learn that this is never permitted inside, not in your home and certainly not in anyone else's.

Urine-marks are usually found on vertical surfaces, such as the back of a sofa, a door, or a tall houseplant. Dogs who haven't been spayed or neutered are more likely to urine-mark, but altered dogs may take up the habit if they believe their territory is threatened.

The most common reasons dogs urine-mark include new animals in the home (your friend brings her dog over or you get a new puppy), conflicts with other animals in the home, unfamiliar objects in the dog's environment such as luggage or handbags belonging to visitors, and items that smell strange or have another animal's scent on them. All

of these unfamiliar scents can trigger in Duke the need to
assert that this is his place. Urine-marking in the house is a

behavior problem rather than a house-training accident and should be dealt with accordingly.

What's the best way to handle urine-marking? If you don't plan to breed or show your dog, have him or her neutered or spayed at or before sexual maturity (usually six to nine months of age, depending on the breed and the individual dog). Spaying and neutering can also help the problem in older animals, although it may take longer for them to break the habit of marking.

A bellyband on a male dog can also help prevent mark-ing behavior. Bellybands are worn low on the dog's belly and cover the end of the penis so the dog can't mark. Your dog should wear a bellyband anytime you can't supervise him, or anytime he goes to someone's home or a public place such as a hotel.

If a bellyband isn't an option, make it unpleasant for Duke to mark. If he likes to lift his leg on the sofa or on a door, cover the area with aluminum foil. When the urine hits it, the sound will startle your dog, and the urine will probably splash back onto him.

Foil doesn't complement your decor? Take the initiative and put items your dog might mark out of his reach.

Obviously, you can't do that with furniture, so try changing the area so your dog won't want to mark there. Play with him or feed him in that area so he becomes comfortable.

Use an enzymatic cleanser to destroy the odor left by the urine. Avoid those with a strong fragrance; your dog may be tempted to mark over them. If you see your dog start to lift his leg or even sniff an area that he's marked previously, distract him by squeaking a toy or squirting him with a water gun. Reward him with praise if he abandons his plan to mark. When you can't be there to supervise, confine your dog outdoors in a securely fenced run, in a room where he doesn't mark, or in his crate. Prevention is the key to solving most behavior problems.

Duke's unsure of himself because there's a new dog (cat, baby, spouse) in town? Help him make friends with the newcomer by recognizing and supporting the canine pecking order. Duke might have been top dog when it was just him, but now he needs to work out a relationship with the new dog or person. Let it happen on the dog's terms. Just because Duke is older, bigger, or your favorite doesn't necessarily mean that he will automatically be the alpha dog. Oftentimes it's the little dogs who are in charge. Serious fights, however, indicate that a behaviorist's help is needed.

If the newcomer is a person, Duke needs to become familiar with him or her. A spouse or older child can take on the responsibility of feeding, grooming, or training Duke. A baby can't do that, but you can give Duke treats when he gently sniffs the baby or behaves calmly in his or her presence. In Duke's mind, Baby should equal Good Things.

Lastly, establish your own leadership. If Duke recognizes that you're in charge, he won't feel the need to mark territory. Avoid punishing your dog for urine-marking unless you catch him in the act. Instead, work to understand why he's marking so you can resolve the problem.

The Eleven Commandments of Good Dog Ownership

One of the best things you can have in life is a happy, successful relationship with your dog. To your dog, you are the leader she can always count on to keep her safe, fed, and cared for. To you, your dog is the best friend who always listens to your problems and concerns. The following rules are your guide to forging this special friendship.

1. Train your dog. Be consistent and build on her strengths while understanding her limitations.

2. Never hit your dog or punish her after the fact.

3. Play with and exercise your dog every day.

4. Don't leave your dog alone for extended periods of time.

5. Feed your dog high-quality food and give her fresh water daily.

6. Supply clean and comfortable dog bedding for your dog's relaxation and sleep.

7. Never expose your dog to extreme heat or cold for long periods of time.

8. Pick up after your dog.

9. Provide your dog with regular veterinary care and grooming.

10. Never let your dog be a nuisance to the neighborhood by barking nonstop or roaming unsupervised.

11. Treat your dog as a beloved family member.

Kim Campbell Thornton is an award-winning writer and editor. During her tenure as editor of *Dog Fancy*, the magazine won three Dog Writers Association of America Maxwell Awards for best all-breed magazine. Her book *Why Do Cats Do That?* was named best behavior book in 1997 by the Cat Writers Association. Kim is the author of *Barking*, *Chewing*, *Digging*, *House-Training*, and *Aggression*. She serves on the DWAA Board of Governors and on the board of the Dog Writers Educational Trust. She is also the former president of the Cat Writers Association.

Buck Jones's humorous illustrations have appeared in numerous magazines (including *Dog Fancy* and *Cat Fancy*) and books. He is the illustrator for the best-selling books *Barking*, *Chewing*, *Digging*, *House-Training*, *Aggression*, *Why Do Cockatiels Do That?*, *Why Do Parakeets Do That?*, *Kittens! Why Do They Do What They Do?*, and *Puppies! Why Do They Do What They Do?*.

For more authoritative and fun facts about dogs, including health-care advice, grooming tips, training advice, and insights into the special joys and overcoming the unique problems of dog ownership check out the latest copy of *Dog Fancy* magazine or visit the Web site at www.dogfancy.com.

BowTie Press is a division of BowTie, Inc., which is the world's largest publisher of pet magazines. For more books on dog behavior, look for *Barking, Chewing, Digging, House-Training, Aggression, Dogs Are Better Than Cats, Dogs Rule!, The Splendid Little Book of All Things Dog, Why Do Dogs Do That?* and *Puppies! Why Do They Do What They Do?* You can find all these books and more at www.bowtiepress.com.